# Introduction

Welcome to Learn-a-Language Spanish!

With the aid of these books, students can easily obtain a working knowledge of beginning Spanish. Learning common vocabulary and phrases, then proceeding to verbs and sentence construction gives students the opportunity to learn by themselves with minimum help from adults.

The Spanish language has a consistent spelling and pronunciation pattern. Some marks and accents occur that we don't have in English. The accent mark is a signal that the syllable is to be stressed. All words in Spanish have a "natural" accent that usually occurs in the next to last syllable. The phonetic guide that accompanies many of the words in Spanish will help in both pronunciation and in accenting the proper syllables. The stressed syllable will appear in **bold** type.

The following pronunciation guide will help with Spanish sounds.

| Vowels | How to Pronounce | English Sample |
|---|---|---|
| a | ah | Open wide and say "ah." |
| e | eh | <u>e</u>gg |
| i | ee | s<u>ee</u> |
| o | oh | <u>o</u>nly |
| u | oo | b<u>oo</u>t |

Consonants

The consonants are pronounced much like those in English with the following exceptions:

| h | always silent | |
| j | h | <u>h</u>at |
| qu | k | <u>k</u>ite |
| ll (double l) | y | <u>y</u>et |

This series includes words, phrases, sentences, puzzles, games, and an easy-reference vocabulary list.

Becoming fluent in any language requires practice. Encourage students to name objects at home and at school in Spanish and to try their new skill with Spanish-speaking people they may know.

Nombre (Name) _____
*(**nohm**-breh)*

# The House/La Casa
*(la **kah**-sah)*

Read the word. Say it aloud. Write the word and say it again as you write it.
El (ehl) or la (lah) before a word means "the."

la casa
*(**kah**-sah)* _____

la puerta
*(poo-**ehr**-tah)* _____

la ventana
*(ven-**tah**-nah)* _____

el techo
*(**teh**-choh)* _____

la chimenea
*(chee-meh-**neh**-ah)* _____

el garaje
*(gah-**rah**-heh)* _____

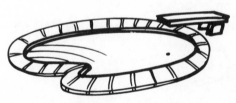

la piscina
*(pee-**see**-nah)* _____

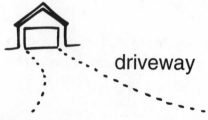

driveway

la entrada de coche
*(ehn-**trah**-dah deh **koh**-cheh)* _____

_____

# In the House/En la Casa

*(ehn lah **kah**-sah)*

Write the Spanish word for each picture.

_____

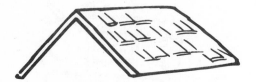

_____

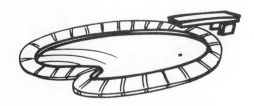

_____

_____

FS-23101 Spanish—Elementary Level 1

# The Living Room/La Sala
## (la **sah**-lah)

Read the word. Say it aloud. Write the word and say it again as you write it.

el sillón
*(see-**yohn**)* _____

la televisión
*(teh-leh-vee-**syohn**)* _____

el sofá
*(so-**fah**)* _____

la radio
*(**rah**-deeoh)* _____

la lámpara
*(**lahm**-pah-rah)* _____

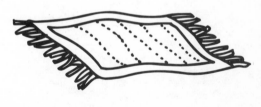

la alfombra
*(ahl-**fohm**-brah)* _____

el teléfono
*(teh-**leh**-foh-noh)* _____

las cortinas
*(kohr-**tee**-nahs)* _____

4

# The Living Room/La Sala

Draw a line between each word and its matching picture.

la sofá

la alfombra

el sillón

las cortinas

la lámpara

la televisión

la radio

# The Kitchen/La Cocina
## *(koh-**see**-nah)*

Read the word. Say it aloud. Write the word and say it again as you write it.

la estufa
*(ehs-**too**-fah)* _____

la tostadora
*(tohs-tah-**doh**-rah)* _____

el refrigerador
*(reh-free-heh-**rah**-dohr)* _____

el horno
*(**ohr**-noh)* _____

la sartén
*(sahr-**tehn**)* _____

el gabinete
*(gah-bee-**neh**-teh)* _____

la olla
*(**oh**-yah)* _____

la lavadora de platos
*(lah-vah-**doh**-rah deh **plah**-tohs)* _____

la licuadora
*(lee-kwah-**doh**-rah)* _____

el reloj
*(reh-**loh**)* _____

FS-23101 Spanish—Elementary Level 1

# La Cocina

Label the parts of the kitchen in Spanish.

FS-23101 Spanish—Elementary Level 1

# The Dining Room/El Comedor
## (koh-**meh**-dohr)

Read the word. Say it aloud. Write the word and say it again as you write it.

la mesa
(**meh**-sah) _____

el plato
(**plah**-toh) _____

la silla
(**see**-yah) _____

la taza
(**tah**-sah) _____

la cuchara
(coo-**chah**-rah) _____

los platos
(**plah**-tohs) _____

el cuchillo
(coo-**chee**-yoh) _____

el mantel
(mahn-**tehl**) _____

el tenedor
(teh-neh-**dore**) _____

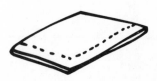

la servilleta
(sehr-vee-**yeh**-tah) _____

FS-23101 Spanish—Elementary Level 1

# The Dining Room/El Comedor

Read the words. Say them aloud. Draw each item on the table and label it.

| | | | |
|---|---|---|---|
| el plato | el tenedor | el cuchillo | la silla |
| la servilleta | la cuchara | el mantel | la taza |

# The Bathroom/El Baño
### (**bah**-nyoh)

Read the word. Say it aloud. Write the word and say it again as you write it.

**el baño**
(**bah**-nyoh) _____

**el jabón**
(hah-**bohn**) _____

**la tina**
(**tee**-nah) _____

**la ducha**
(**doo**-chah) _____

**el lavabo**
(lah-**vah**-boh) _____

**el papel higiénico**
(pah-**pehl** ee-**hyehn**-ee-koh) _____

_____

**la toalla**
(toh-**ah**-yah) _____

**el champú**
(chahm-**poo**) _____

FS-23101 Spanish—Elementary Level 1

# The Bathroom/El Baño

Label the parts of the bathroom in Spanish. Draw the two other bathroom items you know and label them too.

# The Bedroom/La Recámara
## (reh-**kah**-mah-rah)

Read the word. Say it aloud. Write the word and say it again as you write it.

la cama
(**kah**-mah) _____

el armario
(ahr-**mah**-ryoh) _____

la almohada
(ahl-moh-**ah**-dah) _____

la cobija
(koh-**bee**-hah) _____

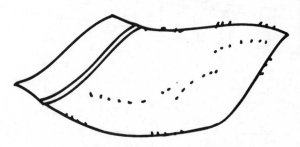

la sábana
(**sah**-bah-nah) _____

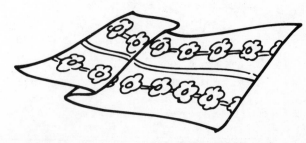

# In the Closet/Dentro del Armario
### (**dehn**-troh dehl ahr-**mah**-r'yoh)

Read the word. Say it aloud. Write the word and say it again as you write it.

los pantalones
*(pahn-tah-**loh**-nehs)* _____

los zapatos
*(sah-**pah**-tohs)* _____

la camisa
*(kah-**mee**-sah)* _____

las botas
*(**boh**-tahs)* _____

el vestido
*(vehs-**tee**-doh)* _____

el abrigo
*(ah-**bree**-goh)* _____

la blusa
*(**bloo**-sah)* _____

el suéter
*(**sweh**-tehr)* _____

la falda
*(**fahl**-dah)* _____

la chaqueta
*(chah-**keh**-tah)* _____

13

# The Bedroom/La Recámara
# In the Closet/Dentro del Armario

Read each word, then say it aloud. Draw a picture of each word and put them all in a scene.

la cama            la almohada            los zapatos

los pantalones            el armario

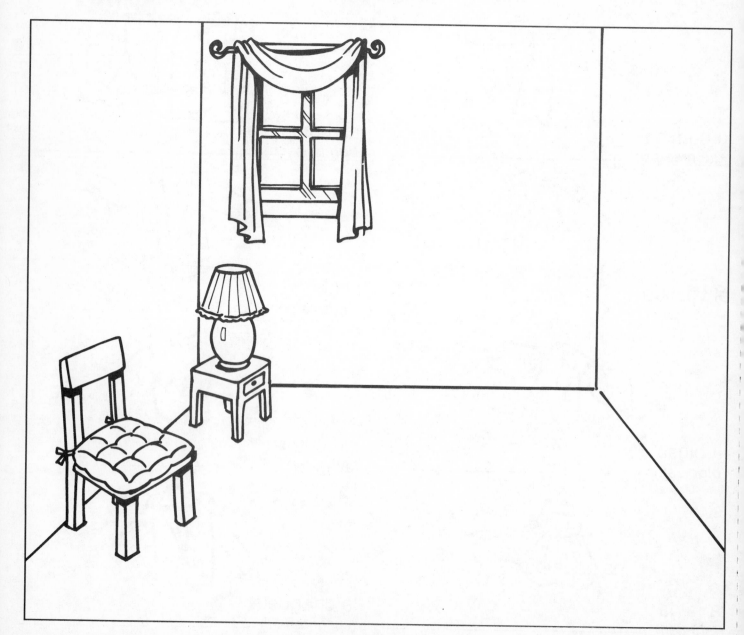

# In the Closet/Dentro del Armario

Draw a line between each word and its matching picture.

la blusa

las botas

la sábana

el vestido

la cobija

la falda

el sueter

los zapatos

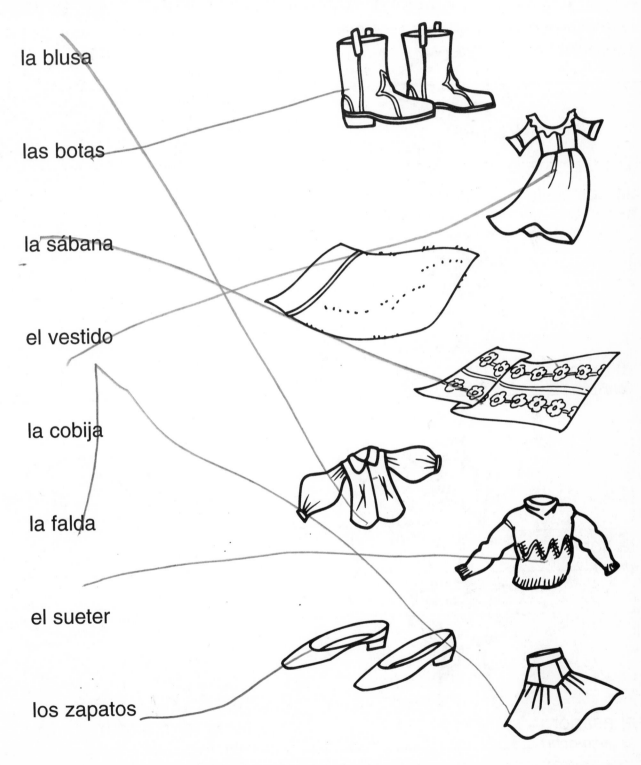

FS-23101 Spanish—Elementary Level 1

# The Garden/El Jardín
## (hahr-**deen**)

Read the word. Say it aloud. Write the word and say it again as you write it.

la sombrilla
*(sohm-**bree**-yah)* _____

las plantas
*(**plahn**-tahs)* _____

el árbol
*(**ahr**-bohl)* _____

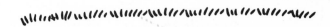

el césped
*(**sehs**-ped)* _____

la flor
*(flohr)* _____

la manguera
*(mahn-**geh**-rah)* _____

el asador
*(ah-**sah**-dohr)* _____

la tierra (dirt, earth)
*(tee-**eh**-rah)* _____

16

# The Garden/El Jardín

Draw a line between each word and its matching picture.

la flor

el césped

el árbol

la sombrilla

la manguera

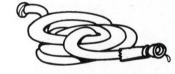

las plantas

la tierra

el asador

FS-23101 Spanish—Elementary Level 1

Nombre (Name) _____

# Around the House/Dentro de la Casa
## (*dehn*-troh)

Draw a scene of a house that includes the following things:

| chimenea | ventana | techo | sombrilla | silla |
|----------|---------|-------|-----------|-------|
| flor | puerta | asador | mesa | árbol |

# Around the House/Dentro de la Casa

Write the names of five rooms in the house. Draw two things found in each room and write their names. Say the words.

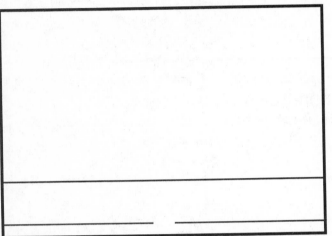

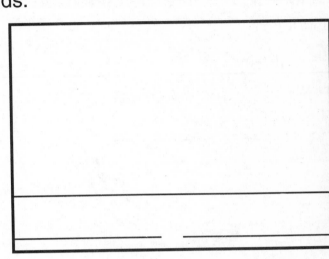

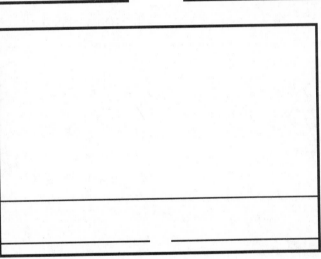

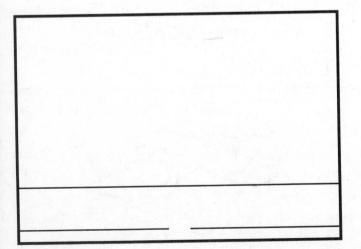

# Colors/Los Colores

## (koh-**loh**-rehs)

Read the word. Say it aloud. Write the word and say it again as you write it. Color each picture the correct color.

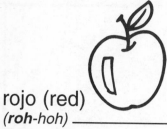

rojo (red)
(**roh**-hoh) _____

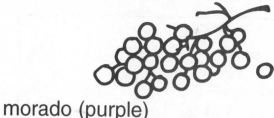

morado (purple)
(moh-**rah**-doh) _____

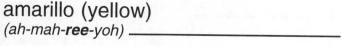

amarillo (yellow)
(ah-mah-**ree**-yoh) _____

café (brown)
(kah-**feh**) _____

verde (green)
(**vehr**-deh) _____

negro (black)
(**neh**-groh) _____

azul (blue)
(ah-**sool**) _____

blanco (white)
(**blahn**-koh) _____

anaranjado (orange)
(ah-nah-rahn-**hah**-doh) _____

rosado (pink)
(roh-**sah**-doh) _____

# Colors/Los Colores

Color each picture, then draw a line between each word and its matching picture.

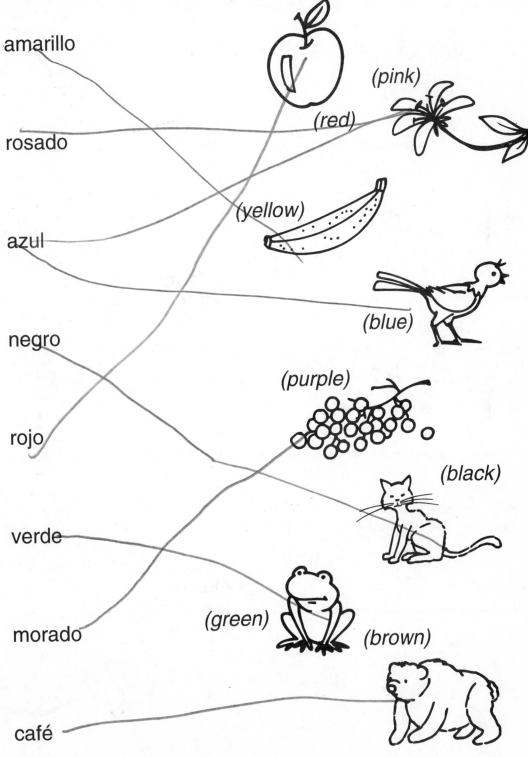

amarillo

rosado

azul

negro

rojo

verde

morado

café

*(pink)*

*(red)*

*(yellow)*

*(blue)*

*(purple)*

*(black)*

*(green)*

*(brown)*

# Numbers/Los Números 1-10

## *(noo-meh-rohs)*

Read the word. Say it aloud. Write the word and say it again as you write it.

uno
*(oo-noh)* _____

seis
*(seh-ees)* _____

dos
*(dohs)* _____

tres
*(trehs)* _____

cuatro
*(kwah-troh)* _____

cinco
*(seen-koh)* _____

siete
*(syeh-teh)* _____

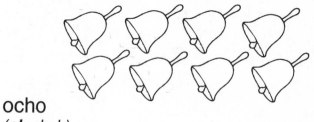

ocho
*(oh-choh)* _____

nueve
*(noo-eh-veh)* _____

diez
*(dyehs)* _____

FS-23101 Spanish—Elementary Level 1

Nombre (Name) _____

# Numbers/Los Números 11-20

## *(noo-*meh-rohs)*

Read the word. Say it aloud. Write the word and say it again as you write it.

once
*(**ohn**-seh)* _____

diez y seis
*(dyehs ee **seh**-ees)* _____

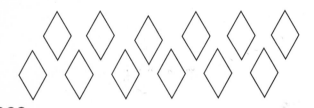

doce
*(**doh**-seh)* _____

diez y siete
*(dyehs ee **syeh**-teh)* _____

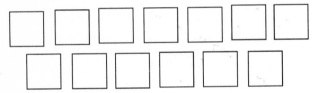

trece
*(**treh**-seh)* _____

diez y ocho
*(dyehs ee **oh**-choh)* _____

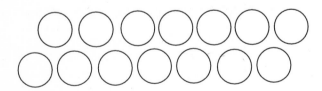

catorce
*(kah-**tohr**-seh)* _____

diez y nueve
*(dyehs ee noo-**eh**-veh)* _____

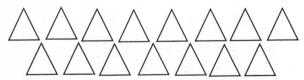

quince
*(**keen**-seh)* _____

veinte
*(**vain**-teh)* _____

         FS-23101 Spanish—Elementary Level 1

# Number Words/Palabras de Números

Write the number word for each set of objects.

_____

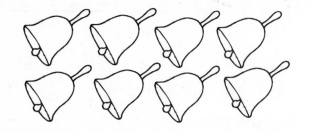

_____

_____

_____

_____

_____

FS-23101 Spanish—Elementary Level 1

Nombre (Name) _____

# Shapes/Las Formas
## (*fohr*-mahs)

Read the word. Say it aloud. Write the word and say it again as you write it.

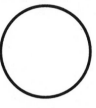

el círculo
(*seehr*-coo-loh) _____

el corazón
(koh-rah-*sohn*) _____

el triángulo
(tree-*ahn*-goo-loh) _____

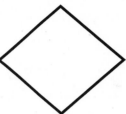

el diamante
(dee-ah-*mahn*-teh) _____

el cuadrado
(kwah-*drah*-doh) _____

la estrella
(ehs-*treh*-yah) _____

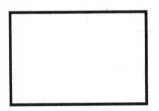

el rectángulo
(reck-*tahn*-goo-loh) _____

el cono
(*koh*-noh) _____

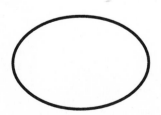

el óvalo
(*oh*-vah-loh) _____

el hexágono
(eks-*ah*-goh-noh) _____

# Shapes/Las Formas

Draw a picture for each Spanish word to show the following shapes:

el círculo

el cuadrado

el cono

el diamante

la estrella

# Shapes and Numbers/Formas y Números

Read about the shapes. Draw the correct number and color.

tres corazones rojos

dos triángulos verdes

cinco cuadrados morados

diez diamantes azules

ocho estrellas blancas

 FS-23101 Spanish—Elementary Level 1

# The Family/La Familia
## *(fah-**mee**-lyah)*

Read the word. Say it aloud. Write the word and say it again as you write it.

la mamá
*(mah-**mah**)* _____

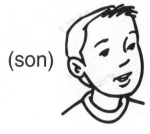

(son)

el hijo
*(**ee**-hoh)* _____

el papá
*(pah-**pah**)* _____

(daughter)

la hija
*(**ee**-hah)* _____

(brother)

el hermano
*(ehr-**mah**-noh)* _____

(grandfather)

el abuelo
*(ah-**bweh**-loh)* _____

(sister)

la hermana
*(ehr-**mah**-nah)* _____

(grandmother)

la abuela
*(ah-**bweh**-lah)* _____

FS-23101 Spanish—Elementary Level 1

# Family Members/Miembros de la Familia
## (mee-**ehm**-brohs)

Read the word. Say it aloud. Write the word and say it again as you write it.

**el bebé**
*(beh-**beh**)* _____

(nephew)

**el sobrino**
*(soh-**bree**-noh)* _____

(uncle)

**el tío**
*(**tee**-oh)* _____

 (niece)

**la sobrina**
*(soh-**bree**-nah)* _____

(aunt)

**la tía**
*(**tee**-ah)* _____

(godfather)

**el padrino**
*(pah-**dree**-noh)* _____

(cousin)

**el primo**
*(**pree**-moh)* _____

(godmother)

**la madrina**
*(mah-**dree**-nah)* _____

(cousin)

**la prima**
*(**pree**-mah)* _____

29

# People in the Family/Gente en la Familia
### (*hen*-teh en lah fah-*meel*-yah)

Draw lines to match each picture to the correct family member.

(grandmother)

(mother)

el hermano

el primo

(brother)

(niece)

la tía

el abuelo

(baby)

la mamá

(aunt)

(godmother)

la abuela

el bebé

(cousin)

la madrina

(daughter)

la hija

la sobrina

(grandfather)

FS-23101 Spanish—Elementary Level 1

# Parts of the Body/Partes del Cuerpo
### (*pahr*-tehs dehl *kwehr*-poh)

Read the word. Say it aloud. Write the word and say it again as you write it.

la cabeza
*(kah-**beh**-sah)* _____

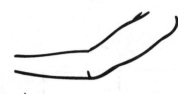

el brazo (arm)
*(**brah**-soh)* _____

la oreja
*(oh-**reh**-hah)* _____

la mano
*(**mah**-noh)* _____

la boca (mouth)
*(**boh**-kah)* _____

el dedo
*(**deh**-doh)* _____

la nariz
*(nah-**rees**)* _____

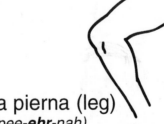

la pierna (leg)
*(pee-**ehr**-nah)* _____

el ojo
*(**oh**-hoh)* _____

el pie
*(pee-**eh**)* _____

Nombre (Name) _____

# The Body/El Cuerpo

Label the body parts in Spanish.

# Words and Pictures/Palabras y Dibujos

Write the Spanish word for each picture.

_____

_____

_____

_____

_____

_____

_____

_____

_____

_____

FS-23101 Spanish—Elementary Level 1

# The Family and Parts of the Body
# La Familia y las Partes del Cuerpo

Draw a picture to show the meaning of each Spanish word.

| | |
|---|---|
| el papá | el pie |
| el bebé | la boca |
| el tío | la pierna |
| la madrina | el hijo |
| la nariz | el dedo |

34

# The School/La Escuela
## (ehs-**kweh**-lah)

Read the word. Say it aloud. Write the word and say it again as you write it.

**el libro**
*(**lee**-broh)* _____

**el salón de clase**
*(sah-**lohn** deh **klah**-seh)* _____

**el lápiz**
*(**lah**-pees)* _____

**la regla**
*(**reh**-glah)* _____

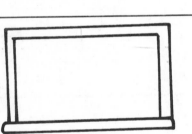

**la pizarra**
*(pee-**sah**-rah)* _____

**la bandera**
*(bahn-**deh**-rah)* _____

**la tiza**
*(**tee**-sah)* _____

**las tijeras**
*(tee-**heh**-rahs)* _____

**el papel**
*(pah-**pehl**)* _____

**el borrador**
*(boh-rah-**dohr**)* _____

FS-23101 Spanish—Elementary Level 1

# Things in School/Cosas en la Escuela

*(koh-sahs)*

Draw a picture for each word.

el libro

el papel

la pizarra

la bandera

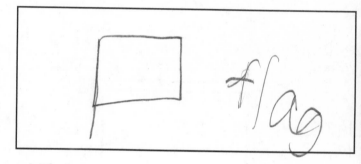

las tijeras

el lápiz

la regla

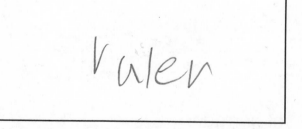

la tiza

FS-23101 Spanish—Elementary Level 1

# People in the School/Gente en la Escuela
## (*hehn*-teh ehn lah ehs-*kweh*-lah)
Read the word. Say it aloud. Write the word and say it again as you write it.

(student)

el/la estudiante
(*ehs-too-dee-yahn-teh*) _____

(girl)

la niña
(*nee-nyah*) _____

(teacher)

la maestra
(*mah-ehs-trah*) _____

(principal)

el director
(*dee-rehk-tohr*) _____

(teacher)

el maestro
(*mah-ehs-troh*) _____

(principal)

la directora
(*dee-rehk-toh-rah*) _____

(boy)

el niño
(*nee-nyoh*) _____

(nurse)

la enfermera
(*ehn-feh-meh-rah*) _____

# Parts of the School/Partes de la Escuela
### (*pahr*-tes deh lah es-**kweh**-lah)

Read the word. Say it aloud. Write the word and say it again as you write it.

la cafetería
*(kah-feh-teh-**ree**-ah)* _____

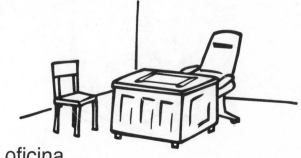

la oficina
*(oh-fee-**see**-nah)* _____

(nurse's office)

la oficina de la enfermera
*(ehn-fehr-**meh**-rah)* _____

el auditorio
*(au-dee-**toh**-ree-oh)* _____

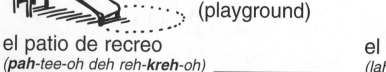

(playground)

el patio de recreo
*(**pah**-tee-oh deh reh-**kreh**-oh)* _____

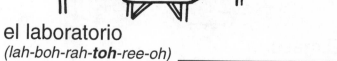

el laboratorio
*(lah-boh-rah-**toh**-ree-oh)* _____

(library)

la biblioteca
*(bee-blee-oh-**teh**-kah)* _____

_____

(classroom)

el salón de clase
*(sah-**lohn** deh **klah**-seh)* _____

_____

FS-23101 Spanish—Elementary Level 1

# Pictures of the School/Dibujos de la Escuela

Label the pictures.

# In the School/En la Escuela

Draw a line to match each picture with the correct word.

la maestra

el salón de clase

la pizarra

la enfermera

la biblioteca

el borrador

el patio de recreo

el libro

la estudiante

el director

Nombre (Name) _____

# The Calendar/El Calendario

*(kah-lehn-**dah**-reeyoh)*

Read the word. Say it aloud. Write the word and say it again as you write it.

Days
Los Días
*(**dee**-ahs)* _____

Monday
lunes
*(**loo**-nehs)* _____

Tuesday
martes
*(**mahr**-tehs)* _____

Friday
viernes
*(vee-**ehr**-nehs)* _____

Wednesday
miércoles
*(mee-**ehr**-koh-lehs)* _____

Saturday
sábado
*(**sah**-bah-doh)* _____

Thursday
jueves
*(**hueh**-ves)* _____

Sunday
domingo
*(doh-**meen**-goh)* _____

FS-23101 Spanish—Elementary Level 1

# The Days of the Week/Los Dias de la Semana
## (seh-**mah**-nah)

Match each day in English to the word in Spanish by drawing a line between each pair.

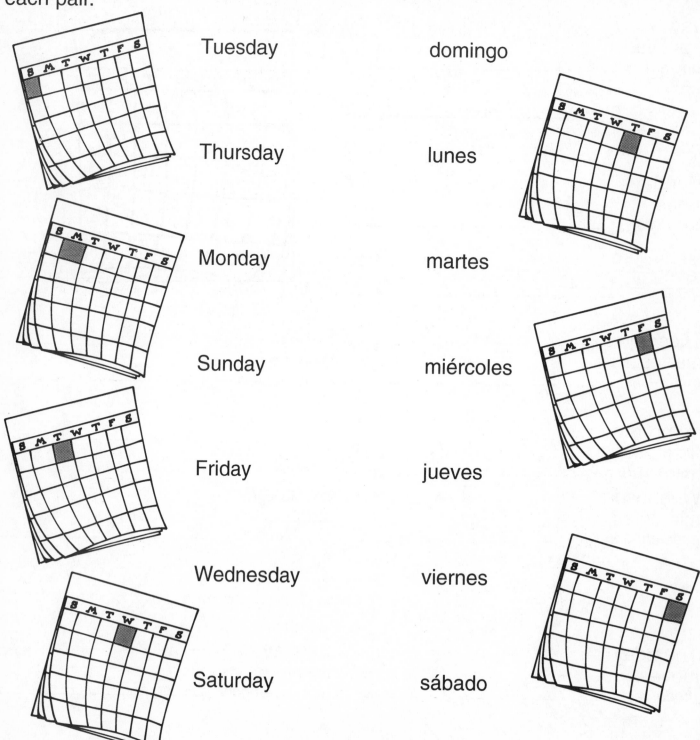

| | |
|---|---|
| Tuesday | domingo |
| Thursday | lunes |
| Monday | martes |
| Sunday | miércoles |
| Friday | jueves |
| Wednesday | viernes |
| Saturday | sábado |

FS-23101 Spanish—Elementary Level 1

# Times of the Day
# Tiempos del Día
*(tee-**em**-pohs dehl **dee**-ah)*

Read each word. Say it aloud. Write the word and say it again as you write it.

today
hoy
*(oy)* _____

yesterday
ayer
*(ah-**yehr**)* _____

tomorrow
mañana
*(mah-**nyah**-nah)* _____

afternoon
tarde
*(**tahr**-deh)* _____

morning
mañana
*(mah-**nyah**-nah)* _____

night
noche
*(**noh**-cheh)* _____

FS-23101 Spanish—Elementary Level 1

Nombre (Name) _____

# Yesterday, Today, and Tomorrow
# Ayer, Hoy, y Mañana

Write the missing days of the week.
Example:

| domingo | lunes | martes |
| --- | --- | --- |
| ayer | hoy | mañana |

| _____ | martes | _____ |
| --- | --- | --- |
| ayer | hoy | mañana |

| _____ | miércoles | _____ |
| --- | --- | --- |
| ayer | hoy | mañana |

| _____ | viernes | _____ |
| --- | --- | --- |
| ayer | hoy | mañana |

| _____ | domingo | _____ |
| --- | --- | --- |
| ayer | hoy | mañana |

| _____ | sábado | _____ |
| --- | --- | --- |
| ayer | hoy | mañana |

| _____ | jueves | _____ |
| --- | --- | --- |
| ayer | hoy | mañana |

# My Day/Mi Día

Draw a scene to show two things you might do at each time of day.

mañana



noche



tarde

# The Months/Los Meses

## *(mehs-ehs)*

Read the word. Say it aloud. Write the word and say it again as you write it.

January      enero
*(e-**neh**-roh)*     _____

February     febrero
*(feh-**breh**-roh)*    _____

March       marzo
*(**mahr**-soh)*      _____

April        abril
*(ah-**breel**)*      _____

May        mayo
*(**mah**-yoh)*      _____

June       junio
*(**hoo**-nyoh)*     _____

July        julio
*(**hoo**-lyoh)*      _____

August     agosto
*(ah-**gohs**-toh)*    _____

September   septiembre
*(sehp-**tyehm**-breh)* _____

October     octubre
*(ohk-**too**-breh)*    _____

November   noviembre
*(noh-**vyehm**-breh)* _____

December   diciembre
*(dee-**syehm**-breh)* _____

              FS-23101 Spanish—Elementary Level 1

# Match the Months/Empareja los Meses

## *(ehm-pah-**reh**-hah)*

Match the month in English to the month in Spanish by drawing a line between each pair.

| | |
|---|---|
| March | agosto |
| May | mayo |
| July | febrero |
| August | abril |
| October | marzo |
| December | junio |
| September | julio |
| February | octubre |
| June | septiembre |
| April | diciembre |

FS-23101 Spanish—Elementary Level 1

# The Seasons/Las Estaciones

*(ehs-tah-__syohn__-ehs)*

Read the word. Say it aloud. Write the word and say it again as you write it.

Spring

primavera
*(pree-mah-__veh__-rah)* _____

Summer

verano
*(veh-__rah__-noh)* _____

Fall

otoño
*(oh-__toh__-nyoh)* _____

Winter

invierno
*(een-__vyehr__-noh)* _____

Nombre (Name) _____

# The Seasons/Las Estaciones

Write the name of the season next to each picture. Think of and draw something you would see during each season.

_____

_____

_____

_____

49

FS-23101 Spanish—Elementary Level 1

# Fruits/Las Frutas

## *(froo-tahs)*

Read the word. Say it aloud. Write the word and say it again as you write it.

**naranja**
*(nah-**rahn**-hah)* _____

**melón**
*(meh-**lohn**)* _____

**manzana**
*(mahn-**sah**-nah)* _____

**durazno**
*(doo-**rahs**-noh)* _____

**plátano**
*(**plah**-tah-noh)* _____

**piña**
*(**pee**-nyah)* _____

**pera**
*(**peh**-rah)* _____

**fresa**
*(**freh**-sah)* _____

**uvas**
*(**oo**-vahs)* _____

**limón**
*(lee-**mohn**)* _____

# Fruits/Las Frutas

Write the correct name of each fruit in Spanish.

_____

_____

_____

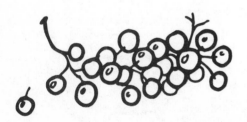

_____

FS-23101 Spanish—Elementary Level 1

Nombre (Name) _____

# Vegetables/Las Legumbres
*(leh-**goom**-brehs)*

Read the word. Say it aloud. Write the word and say it again as you write it.

la zanahoria
*(sah-nah-**oh**-ree-ah)* _____

el maíz
*(mah-**ees**)* _____

la lechuga
*(leh-**choo**-gah)* _____

la papa
*(**pah**-pah)* _____

el pepino
*(peh-**pee**-noh)* _____

la espinaca
*(ehs-pee-**nah**-kah)* _____

los guisantes
*(ghee-**sahn**-tehs)* _____

el tomate
*(toh-**mah**-teh)* _____

Nombre (Name) _____

# Fruits and Vegetables
# Las Frutas y Las Legumbres

Label the fruits and vegetables you see on the table. Write the correct Spanish word on each line next to the right number.

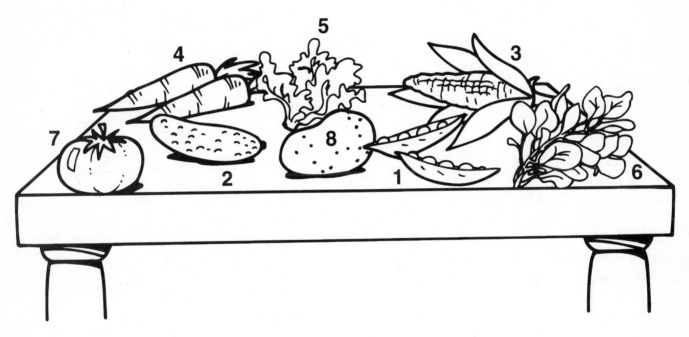

1. _____

2. _____

3. _____

4. _____

5. _____

6. _____

7. _____

8. _____

# Dairy Products/Las Productos Lácteos

*(proh-**dook**-tohs **lahk**-teh-ohs)*

Read the word. Say it aloud. Write the word and say it again as you write it.

la leche
*(**leh**-cheh)* _____

el queso
*(**keh**-soh)* _____

el helado
*(eh-**lah**-doh)* _____

el yogur
*(yoh-**goor**)* _____

la crema
*(**kreh**-mah)* _____

# Favorite Foods/Las Comidas Favoritas

*(koh-**mee**-das fah-voh-**ree**-tahs)*

Draw two each of your favorite fruits, vegetables, and dairy products, then write their names.

frutas

_____

_____

legumbres

_____

_____

productos lácteos

_____

_____

# Breads and Cereals/Los Panes y los Cereales
## (*pah*-nehs *ee seh-reh-ah-lehs*)

Read the word. Say it aloud. Write the word and say it again as you write it.

(toast)

el pan
*(pahn)* _____

el pan tostado
*(pahn tohs-tah-doh)* _____

(pancake)

el pastel
*(pahs-tehl)* _____

el panqueque
*(pahn-queh-queh)* _____

(flour)

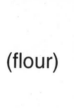

el cereal
*(seh-reh-ahl)* _____

la harina
*(ah-ree-nah)* _____

(cookie)

(rice)

la galleta
*(gah-yeh-tah)* _____

el arroz
*(ah-rohs)* _____

(roll)

la tortilla
*(tohr-tee-yah)* _____

el panecillo
*(pah-neh-see-yoh)* _____

   FS-23101 Spanish—Elementary Level 1

Nombre (Name) _____

# Breads and Cereals/Los Panes y los Cereales

Draw the correct food from the Breads and Cereal group for each word.

| el pastel | la tortilla | el pan |
| la galleta | el panqueque | la harina |
| el pan tostado | el cereal | el arroz |

# Meat/La Carne
## (*kahr*-neh)

Read the word. Say it aloud. Write the word and say it again as you write it.

(chicken)

el pollo
(*poh*-yoh) _____

(ham)

el jamón
(hah-*mohn*) _____

el pescado
(pehs-*kah*-doh) _____

(bacon)

el tocino
(toh-*see*-noh) _____

(beef)

la carne de res
(*kahr*-neh deh rehs) _____

(pork)

la carne de cerdo
(*kahr*-neh deh *sehr*-doh) _____

_____

la hamburguesa
(ahm-boor-*gheh*-sah) _____

(pork chop)

la chuleta de cerdo
(choo-*leh*-tah deh *sehr*-doh) _____

_____

(sausage)

la salchicha
(sahl-*chee*-chah) _____

(lamb)

la carne de cordero
(*kahr*-neh deh kohr-*deh*-roh) _____

# Other Foods/Las Otras Comidas

## (oh-trahs koh-**mee**-dahs)

Read the word. Say it aloud. Write the word and say it again as you write it.

el dulce
(**dool**-seh) _____

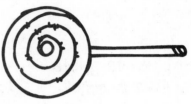

la paleta
(pah-**leh**-tah) _____

la soda
(**soh**-dah) _____

la crema de cacahuate
(**kreh**-mah deh kah-kah-**wah**-teh) _____

la mantequilla
(mahn-teh-**kee**-yah) _____

el ponche
(**pohn**-cheh) _____

el chicle
(**chee**-kleh) _____

las palomitas de maíz
(pah-loh-**mee**-tahs deh mah-**ees**) _____

el chocolate
(choh-koh-**lah**-teh) _____

el azúcar
(ah-**soo**-kahr) _____

# Breakfast/El Desayuno

## (deh-sah-**yoo**-noh)

Draw a breakfast you like and one you don't like. Write the Spanish word for each word you choose.

|  |  |
|---|---|
| I like/Me gusta | I don't like/No me gusta |
| *(meh-**goos**-tah)* | *(no me **goos**-tah)* |

 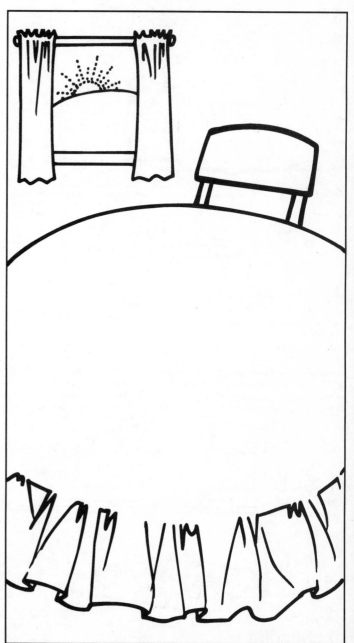

# Lunch/El Almuerzo

## (ahl-*mooehr*-so)

Draw a lunch you would like to eat and write the Spanish word for each item.

# Dinner/La Cena

## *(seh*-na)*

Draw a dinner scene and write the Spanish word for each item.

# Word Search
# Buscando Palabras
## (**boohs**-kahn-doh)

| o | e | c | r | c | n | m | s | l |
|---|---|---|---|---|---|---|---|---|
| d | h | v | s | o | a | p | i | a |
| a | c | m | e | n | j | y | l | p |
| l | e | x | z | n | m | o | l | i |
| e | l | a | a | l | t | a | a | z |
| h | n | s | a | u | o | a | í | x |
| a | a | s | v | j | u | b | n | z |
| c | e | a | x | v | g | m | r | a |
| m | s | e | s | t | u | f | a | á |

Find and circle the Spanish words hidden in the puzzle above.

| | | |
|---|---|---|
| árbol | leche | rojo |
| casa | maíz | silla |
| estufa | manzana | uvas |
| helado | mesa | ventana |
| lapiz | | |

63

Nombre (Name) _____

# Crossword Puzzle/Crucigrama

## (kroo-see-**grah**-mah)

Write the Spanish words in the puzzle.

**Across**
1. table
2. grapes
3. orange
4. corn
6. tree
8. chalkboard
9. blender

**Down**
1. apple
5. strawberry
7. milk
8. cucumber

FS-23101 Spanish—Elementary Level 1

# Crossword Puzzle/ Crucigrama

Write the Spanish words for the words below in the puzzle.

## Across
1. lollipop
2. chocolate
3. sugar
4. gum
5. cookie

## Down
1. cake
6. butter
7. candy
8. soda pop

# REVIEW #1/Repaso #1

*(reh-**pah**-soh)*

Label the things on the table with the correct Spanish words.

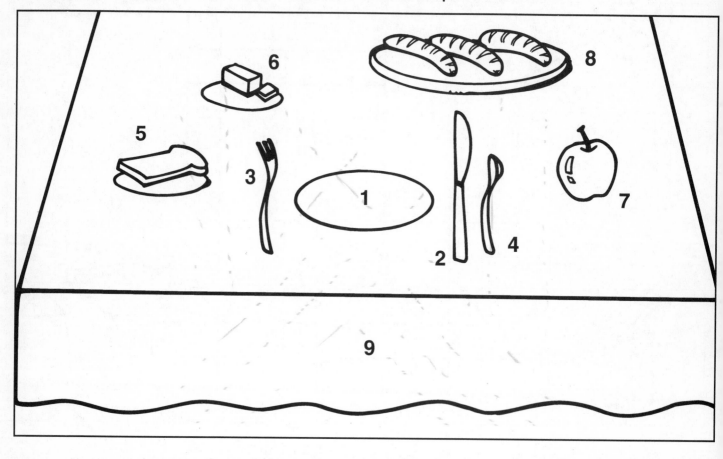

1. _____     6. _____

2. _____     7. _____

3. _____     8. _____

4. _____     9. _____

5. _____

# REVIEW #2/Repaso #2

Label the things on the desk with the correct Spanish words.

1. _____   6. _____

2. _____   7. _____

3. _____   8. _____

4. _____   9. _____

5. _____   10. _____

# REVIEW #3/Repaso #3

Label the pieces of clothing and body parts with the correct Spanish words.

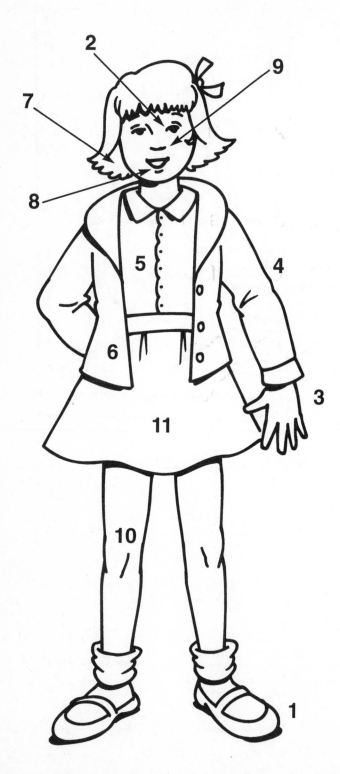

1. _____

2. _____

3. _____

4. _____

5. _____

6. _____

7. _____

8. _____

9. _____

10. _____

11. _____

# Vocabulary Test
# Examen de Vocabulario
## (ehk-**sah**-mehn deh vocah-boo-**lah**-ree-oh)

Circle the best answer.

1. A place where people live

   A. flor          C. mesa
   B. cama          D. casa

2. I use this item to cut my food.

   A. manzana       C. cuchillo
   B. cuchara       D. teléfono

3. She is the person who teaches math.

   A. árbol         C. uvas
   B. maestro       D. maestra

4. A little girl is a…

   A. azúcar        C. pan
   B. niña          D. niño

5. My mother writes with a…
   A. lápiz         C. salchicha
   B. azul          D. libro

6. This plant grows in my garden.

   A. sartén        C. maestra
   B. flor          D. radio

7. Billy has this many sisters.

   A. dos           C. taza
   B. estufa        D. ventana

8. Jose's favorite fruit is

   A. dulce         C. naranja
   B. paleta        D. techo

9. Every Wednesday Sally eats

   A. niña          C. nariz
   B. hamburguesa   D. falda

10. When my sister takes a bath, she washes with…

    A. jabón        C. limón
    B. olla         D. tina

     FS-23101 Spanish—Elementary Level 1

11. If you want to make toast, you will need

A. chimenea     C. tostadora
B. leche        D. puerta

12. Mary was always late for school. Her father bought her

A. casa         C. galleta
B. chicle       D. reloj

13. Mr. Smith uses one of these to write on the board.

A. tiza         C. pepino
B. taza         D. puerta

14. What does not go in a salad?

A. lechuga      C. papel
B. tomate       D. pepino

15. What is not a fruit?

A. carne        C. manzana
B. freza        D. plátano

16. Sam takes a bath in

A. césped       C. techo
B. tina         D. toalla

17. There is ____ in the sky.

A. silla        C. círculo
B. horno        D. estrella

18. Jim's favorite person is his...

A. papá     C. lavadora de
                 platos
B. paleta   D. camisa

19. The season after spring is...

A. primavera    C. otoño
D. invierno     D. verano

20. We ate cake and ___ for my birthday.

A. helado       C. tocino
B. sueter       D. ventana

# Fun With Spanish

1. Concentration Game (Juego de Concentración)
   Make picture cards and word cards of the following:
   colors
   numbers
   shapes
   Place all of the picture cards and word cards facing down. Players take turns turning two cards up to see if they can get a match (picture card and its corresponding word card). If the player does not get a match, then he/she returns the two cards to their original positions facing down. Players continue taking turns until there are no more cards facing down. The player with the most matches wins the game.

2. Go Fish (Ve a Pescar)
   Use the cards from the concentration game to play Go Fish.
   Directions for Go Fish:
   Give seven cards to each player. The players take turns asking for the shapes/colors/numbers in their hand of cards. If their opponents don't have the card they Go Fish and take another card from the pile. The winner is the first one to have no cards left.

3. Old Maid (La Viejita)
   Use the cards from the Concentration Game.
   Directions for Old Maid:
   Make a blank card to be the Old Maid. Draw a funny looking person on it. Pass out all the cards. Players go through their hands and pick out all the pairs and put them to the side. Players then take turns picking cards from each others' hand and putting down the pairs as they get them. The loser is the player left with the Old Maid.

4. Draw a Man (Dibuja un Hombre)
   Use the vocabulary words from this book to play Draw a Man.
   On a piece of paper, draw a line for each letter in a word you will keep secret from your opponent. Your opponent will guess letters, one at a time, in the word. For each incorrect guess your opponent makes, draw a body part, and say it in Spanish. Give your opponent ten tries to guess all of the correct letters in your word or to guess the word. If your opponent fails to guess your secret word in ten tries, or by the time you draw a man, you win the game. Your opponent wins the game if he/she guesses your secret word.

5. Think Fast! (¡Piensa Rapida!)
   Using an egg timer, give yourself 15 seconds to write as many Spanish words as you can that go with the house, the school, food, etc.

     FS-23101 Spanish—Elementary Level 1

# Vocabulary/Vocabulario

## Colors

| | | |
|---|---|---|
| black | negro | *(neh-groh)* |
| blue | azul | *(ah-sool)* |
| brown | café | *(kah-feh)* |
| green | verde | *(vehr-deh)* |
| orange | anaranjado | *(ah-nah-rahn-hah-doh)* |
| pink | rosado | *(roh-sah-doh)* |
| purple | morado | *(moh-rah-doh)* |
| red | rojo | *(roh-hoh)* |
| white | blanco | *(blahn-koh)* |
| yellow | amarillo | *(ah-mah-ree-yoh)* |

## Numbers

| | | |
|---|---|---|
| one | uno | *(oo-noh)* |
| two | dos | *(dohs)* |
| three | tres | *(trehs)* |
| four | cuatro | *(kwah-tro)* |
| five | cinco | *(seen-koh)* |
| six | seis | *(sehs)* |
| seven | siete | *(syeh-teh)* |
| eight | ocho | *(oh-choh)* |
| nine | nueve | *(nweh-veh)* |
| ten | diez | *(dyehs)* |
| eleven | once | *(ohn-seh)* |
| twelve | doce | *(doh-seh)* |
| thirten | trece | *(treh-seh)* |
| fourteen | catorce | *(cah-tohr-seh)* |
| fifteen | quince | *(keen-seh)* |
| sixteen | diez y seis | *(dyehs-ee-sehs)* |
| seventeen | diez y siete | *(dyehs-ee-syeh-teh)* |
| eighteen | diez y ocho | *(dyehs-ee-oh-choh)* |
| nineteen | diez y nueve | *(dyehs-ee-nweh-veh)* |
| twenty | veinte | *(vehn-teh)* |

## Shapes

| | | |
|---|---|---|
| circle | círculo | *(seer-koo-loh)* |
| cone | cono | *(koh-noh)* |
| diamond | diamante | *(dee-ah-mahn-teh)* |
| heart | corazón | *(koh-rah-sohn)* |
| hexagon | hexágono | *(eks-ah-goh-noh)* |
| oval | óvalo | *(oh-vah-loh)* |
| rectangle | rectángulo | *(rehk-tahn-goo-loh)* |
| square | cuadrado | *(kwah-drah-doh)* |
| star | estrella | *(ehs-treh-yah)* |
| triangle | triángulo | *(tree-ahn-goo-loh)* |

FS-23101 Spanish—Elementary Level 1

# House

## Parts of the house

| | | |
|---|---|---|
| chimney | chimenea | *(chee-meh-**neh**-ah)* |
| door | puerta | *(poo-**ehr**-tah)* |
| garden | jardín | *(hahr-**deen**)* |
| house | casa | *(**kah**-sah)* |
| roof | techo | *(**teh**-choh)* |
| window | ventana | *(vehn-**tah**-nah)* |

## Rooms in the house

| | | |
|---|---|---|
| bathroom | baño | *(**bah**-nyoh)* |
| bedroom | recámara | *(reh-**kah**-mah-rah)* |
| dining room | comedor | *(koh-meh-**dohr**)* |
| kitchen | cocina | *(koh-**see**-nah)* |
| living room | sala | *(**sah**-lah)* |

## Things in the house

| | | |
|---|---|---|
| armchair | sillón | *(see-**yohn**)* |
| bathtub | tina | *(**tee**-nah)* |
| bed | cama | *(**kah**-mah)* |
| blanket | cobija | *(koh-**bee**-hah)* |
| blender | licuadora | *(lee-kwah-**doh**-rah)* |
| chair | silla | *(**see**-yah)* |
| clock | reloj | *(re-**loh**)* |
| closet | armario | *(ahr-**mah**-ryoh)* |
| cover | cobija | *(koh-**bee**-hah)* |
| cup | taza | *(**tah**-sah)* |
| cupboard | gabinete | *(gah-bee-**neh**-teh)* |
| dishes | platos | *(**plah**-tohs)* |
| dishwasher | lavadora de platos | *(lah-vah-**doh**-rah deh **plah**-tohs)* |
| fork | tenedor | *(teh-neh-**dohr**)* |
| frying pan | sartén | *(sahr-**tehn**)* |
| glass | vaso | *(**vah**-soh)* |
| knife | cuchillo | *(koo-**chee**-yoh)* |
| lamp | lámpara | *(**lahm**-pah-rah)* |
| napkin | servilleta | *(sehr-vee-**yeh**-tah)* |
| oven | horno | *(**ohr**-noh)* |
| pillow | almohada | *(ahl-moh-**ah**-dah)* |
| plate | plato | *(**plah**-toh)* |
| pot | olla | *(**oh**-yah)* |
| refrigerator | refrigerador | *(reh-free-heh-**rah**-dohr)* |
| rug | alfombra | *(ahl-**fohm**-brah)* |
| sheet | sábana | *(**sah**-bah-nah)* |
| shower | ducha | *(**doo**-chah)* |
| sink | lavabo | *(lah-**vah**-boh)* |
| soap | jabón | *(hah-**bohn**)* |
| sofa | sofá | *(soh-**fah**)* |
| spoon | cuchara | *(koo-**chah**-rah)* |
| stove | estufa | *(ehs-**too**-fah)* |
| table | mesa | *(**meh**-sah)* |

| | | |
|---|---|---|
| tablecloth | mantel | *(mahn-**tehl**)* |
| television | televisión | *(teh-leh-vee-**syohn**)* |
| toaster | tostadora | *(tohs-tah-**doh**-rah)* |
| towel | toalla | *(toh-**ah**-yah)* |
| wardrobe | ropero | *(ahr-**mah**-ryoh)* |

## Things in the Garden

| | | |
|---|---|---|
| barbeque | asador | *(ah-**sah**-dohr)* |
| dirt, earth | tierra | *(tee-**eh**-rah)* |
| flower | flor | *(flohr)* |
| grass | césped | *(**sehs**-ped)* |
| hose | manguera | *(mahn-**geh**-rah)* |
| plants | plantas | *(**plahn**-tahs)* |
| tree | árbol | *(**ahr**-bohl)* |
| umbrella | sombrilla | *(sohm-**bree**-yah)* |

## Clothing

| | | |
|---|---|---|
| blouse | blusa | *(**bloo**-sah)* |
| boots | botas | *(**boh**-tahs)* |
| coat | abrigo | *(ah-**bree**-goh)* |
| dress | vestido | *(vehs-**tee**-doh)* |
| jacket | chaqueta | *(chah-**keh**-tah)* |
| pants | pantalones | *(pahn-tah-**loh**-nehs)* |
| shirt | camisa | *(kah-**mee**-sah)* |
| shoes | zapatos | *(sah-**pah**-tohs)* |
| skirt | falda | *(**fahl**-dah)* |
| sweater | sueter | *(**sweh**-tehr)* |

## People in the family

| | | |
|---|---|---|
| aunt, uncle | tía, tío | *(**tee**-ah, **tee**-oh)* |
| baby | bebé | *(beh-**beh**)* |
| brother, sister | hermano, hermana | *(ehr-**mah**-noh, ehr-**mah**-nah)* |
| daughter, son | hija, hijo | *(**ee**-hah, **ee**-hoh)* |
| mother, father | mamá, papá | *(mah-**mah**, pah-**pah**)* |
| grandfather | abuelo | *(ah-**bweh**-loh)* |
| grandmother | abuela | *(ah-**bweh**-lah)* |
| cousin | prima, primo | *(**pree**-mah, **pree**-moh)* |
| niece, nephew | sobrina, sobrino | *(soh-**bree**-nah, soh-**bree**-noh)* |
| godmother, godfather | madrina, padrino | *(mah-**dree**-nah, pah-**dree**-noh)* |

## Parts of the body

| | | |
|---|---|---|
| arm | brazo | *(**brah**-soh)* |
| ears | orejas | *(oh-**reh**-hahs)* |
| eyes | ojos | *(**oh**-hohs)* |
| finger | dedo | *(**deh**-doh)* |
| foot | pie | *(pee-**eh**)* |
| hand | mano | *(**mah**-noh)* |
| head | cabeza | *(kah-**beh**-sah)* |
| leg | pierna | *(pee-**ehr**-nah)* |
| nose | nariz | *(nah-**rees**)* |
| mouth | boca | *(**boh**-kah)* |

## The School

| book | libro | (**lee**-broh) |
| boy | niño | (nee-**nyoh**) |
| cafeteria | cafetería | (kah-feh-teh-**ree**-ah) |
| chair | silla | (**see**-yah) |
| chalk | tiza | (**tee**-sah) |
| chalkboard | pizarra | (pee-**sah**-rah) |
| classroom | salón de clase | (sah-**lohn** deh **klah**-se) |
| desk | escritorio | (ehs-kree-**toh**-ryoh) |
| eraser | borrador | (boh-rah-**dohr**) |
| female teacher | maestra | (mah-**ehs**-trah) |
| flag | bandera | (bahn-**deh**-rah) |
| girl | niña | (nee-**nyah**) |
| library | biblioteca | (bee-blee-oh-**teh**-kah) |
| male teacher | maestro | (mah-**ehs**-troh) |
| nurse's office | oficina de la enfermera | (oh-fee-**see**-nah deh lah ehn-fehr-**meh**-rah) |
| office | oficina | (oh-fee-**see**-nah) |
| paper | papel | (pah-**pehl**) |
| pencil | lápiz | (**lah**-pees) |
| playground | patio de recreo | (**pah**-tyoh deh reh-**kreh**-oh) |
| ruler | regla | (**reh**-glah) |
| scissors | tijeras | (tee-**heh**-rahs) |
| student | estudiante | (ehs-too-dee-**yahn**-teh) |

## Days of the week

| Monday | lunes | (**loo**-nehs) |
| Tuesday | martes | (**mahr**-tehs) |
| Wednesday | miércoles | (mee-**ehr**-koh-lehs) |
| Thursday | jueves | (**hueh**-vehs) |
| Friday | viernes | (vee-**ehr**-nehs) |
| Saturday | sábado | (**sah**-bah-doh) |
| Sunday | domingo | (doh-**meen**-goh) |

## Months

| January | enero | (e-**neh**-roh) |
| February | febrero | (feh-**breh**-roh) |
| March | marzo | (**mahr**-soh) |
| April | abril | (ah-**breel**) |
| May | mayo | (**mah**-yoh) |
| June | junio | (**hoo**-nyoh) |
| July | julio | (**hoo**-lyoh) |
| August | agosto | (ah-**gohs**-toh) |
| September | septiembre | (sehp-**tyehm**-breh) |
| October | octubre | (ohk-**too**-breh) |
| November | noviembre | (noh-**vyehm**-breh) |
| December | diciembre | (dee-**syehm**-breh) |

## Foods

| apple | manzana | (mahn-**sah**-nah) |

| bacon | tocino | *(toh-**see**-noh)* |
| banana | plátano | *(**plah**-tah-noh)* |
| beef | carne de res | *(**kahr**-neh deh rehs)* |
| bread | pan | *(pahn)* |
| butter | mantequilla | *(mahn-teh-**kee**-yah)* |
| cake | pastel | *(pahs-**tehl**)* |
| candy | dulce | *(**dool**-seh)* |
| carrot | zanahoria | *(san-nah-**oh**-ree-ah)* |
| cereal | cereal | *(seh-reh-**ahl**)* |
| cheese | queso | *(**keh**-soh)* |
| chicken | pollo | *(**poh**-yoh)* |
| chocolate | chocolate | *(choh-koh-**lah**-teh)* |
| corn | maíz | *(mah-**ees**)* |
| cookie | galleta | *(gah-**yeh**-tah)* |
| cream | crema | *(**kreh**-mah)* |
| cucumber | pepino | *(peh-**pee**-noh)* |
| fish | pescado | *(pehs-**kah**-doh)* |
| flour | harina | *(ah-**ree**-nah)* |
| grapes | uvas | *(**oo**-vahs)* |
| gum | chicle | *(**chee**-kleh)* |
| ham | jamón | *(hah-**mohn**)* |
| hamburger | hamburguesa | *(ahm-boor-**gheh**-sah)* |
| ice cream | helado | *(eh-**lah**-doh)* |
| lamb | carne de cordero | *(**kahr**-neh deh kohr-**deh**-roh)* |
| lemon | limón | *(lee-**mohn**)* |
| lettuce | lechuga | *(leh-**choo**-gah)* |
| lollipop | paleta | *(pah-**leh**-tah)* |
| melon | melón | *(meh-**lohn**)* |
| milk | leche | *(**leh**-cheh)* |
| orange | naranja | *(nah-**rahn**-hah)* |
| pancake | panqueque | *(pahn-**queh**-queh)* |
| peach | durazno | *(doo-**rahs**-noh)* |
| peanut butter | crema de cacahuate | *(**kreh**-mah deh kah-kah-**wah**-teh)* |
| pear | pera | *(**peh**-rah)* |
| peas | guisantes | *(ghee-**sahn**-tehs)* |
| pineapple | piña | *(**pee**-nyah)* |
| popcorn | palomitas de maíz | *(pah-loh-**mee**-tahs deh mah-**ees**)* |
| pork | carne de cerdo | *(**kahr**-neh deh **sehr**-doh)* |
| pork chop | chuleta de cerdo | *(choo-**leh**-tah deh **sehr**-doh)* |
| punch | ponche | *(**pohn**-cheh)* |
| rice | arroz | *(ah-**rohs**)* |
| roll | panecillo | *(pah-neh-**see**-yoh)* |
| sausage | salchicha | *(sahl-**chee**-chah)* |
| soda | soda | *(**soh**-dah)* |
| spinach | espinaca | *(ehs-pee-**nah**-kah)* |
| strawberry | fresa | *(**freh**-sah)* |
| sugar | azúcar | *(ah-**soo**-kahr)* |
| toast | pan tostado | *(pahn tohs-**tah**-doh)* |
| tortilla | tortilla | *(tohr-**tee**-yah)* |
| veal | carne de ternera | *(**kahr**-neh deh tehr-**neh**-rah)* |

FS-23101 Spanish—Elementary Level 1